Ghosts

of the

Natchez Trace

The reader should understand that we were able to obtain some of these stories only if we promised to obscure the actual identity of persons and/or property. This required us to occasionally use fictitious names. In such cases, the names of the people and/or the places are not to be confused with actual places or actual persons living or dead.

This book is dedicated to the animals and people who created and used Natchez Trace. From the early animals who roamed from Mississippi to the salt licks in Tennessee, the Indians who followed those trails, and to the later travelers who adapted the Trace as a passageway for their particular needs, Natchez Trace has served many as a path through the countryside. Once wild and wooly, but now tame and beautiful, long may it continue to serve its purpose.

Many dangers lurked around Natchez Trace. Small bands of outlaws preyed upon the travelers the entire length of the trace. There were also at least two large organized gangs. John Murrel led one, known as the Mystic Clan, and had hideouts all along the Trace. Samuel Mason was another notorious gang leader.

TABLE OF CONTENTS

At milepost 266 is the Tupelo Visitor Center. This is also the Natchez Trace Parkway Headquarters. Brochures, maps, and park bulletins are available. Of lesser importance, Tupelo is also the birthplace of someone named Elvis Presley.

FOREWORD

Ghost stories have been a popular part of our culture for a long time. According to some interpretations of the earliest cave drawings, even those people sat around their fires (once fire was discovered) grunting tales of the supernatural. Perhaps they encountered spiritual representations of some unfortunate family member who had been consumed by a hungry predator. When you are ranked several levels down on the food chain, one tends to fervently believe in help from supernatural sources, and friendly ghosts certainly fit that description.

People still like to read, tell, or hear tales of inexplicable events. Super-action heroes in children's comic books are one example; ghost stories supply that same need regardless of age. Since the after-life remains one of our greatest mysteries, it follows that we are intrigued by anything that might provide a glimpse into what lies beyond. Plus, for some reason getting a little bit scared is considered fun, so ghost stories remain a popular form of entertainment for all ages.

An important aspect of any ghost story is its setting. Some stories are set in places we might never get to visit, such as European castles, or Egyptian tombs. The stories in this book are not only set in an accessible location, but one that has so many attractions that it begs to be visited.

As a traveler along Natchez Trace enjoys the scenery and recreational pursuits it offers, they can also keep an eye out for something of a darker nature tied to the history of the Trace. According to many accounts, some of the Trace's earlier guests may still be lurking nearby, eager to do mischief or simply unconsciously appear.

I grew up in Middle Tennessee, spending much of my impressionable youth in an area crossed by the northern portion of Natchez Trace. As such, I have heard some of the mysterious accounts mentioned in this book for most of my life. As in many such stories, there are usually several versions of the tales.

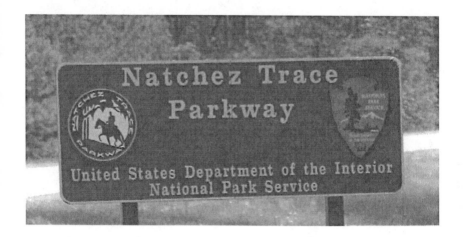

A teller of ghost stories isn't necessarily responsible for the verification of facts. Ghost particulars by nature are usually impossible to prove. Instead, the goal is to present the elements of the tale in an interesting manner, leaving the reader to form their own opinion as to the authenticity of the story.

The following stories are generally offered in the most entertaining version. Most are from legends, hearsay, idle gossip or common folklore. Some, however, are from personal recollections or relayed as told directly to me by someone who actually claimed to have experienced the event.

NATCHEZ TRACE

THIS PLAINLY VISIBLE, THOUGH LONG DESERTED ROAD IS A SECTION OF THE NATCHEZ TRACE, EVOLVED FROM BUFFALO AND INDIAN TRAILS, INTO THE FIRST NATIONAL HIGHWAY OF THE SOUTH-WEST, CUT AND OPENED UNDER AUTHORITY OF THE UNITED STATES GOVERNMENT, AFTER TREATIES NEGOTIATED WITH THE CHICKASAW AND THE CHOCTAW INDIANS, IN 1801.

DESIGNED TO MEET EARLY NECESSITIES OF TRADE BETWEEN NASHVILLE AND THE COUNTRY OF THE LOWER MISSISSIPPI; IT IS AN ABIDING FOOTPRINT OF THE BOLD, CRUDE COMMERCE OF THE PIONEERS: YET IT IS NOT WITHOUT MILITARY SIGNIFICANCE IN THE HISTORY OF OUR COUNTRY. OVER IT PASSED A PART OF ANDREW JACKSON'S ARMY IN HIS CAMPAIGN AGAINST THE CREEK INDIANS IN 1813, AND AGAIN ON HIS RETURN FROM THE BATTLE FIELD OF NEW ORLEANS IN 1815.

BUT, BEFORE TALLEDEGA AND NEW ORLEANS- BEFORE THE SOLDIERS OF JACKSON HAD GIVEN RENOWN TO THE NATCHEZ TRACE, IT RECEIVED ITS IMMORTAL TOUCH OF MELANCHOLY FAME WHEN MERIWETHER LEWIS, JOURNEYING OVER IT ON HIS WAY TO PHILADELPHIA, TO EDIT THE STORY OF HIS GREAT EXPEDITION, HERE MET HIS UNTIMELY DEATH ON THE NIGHT OF OCT. 11, 1809.

INTRODUCTION

The Natchez Trace Parkway is a 444-mile path from Natchez, Mississippi, to near Nashville, Tennessee. The route goes past Jackson and Tupelo, Mississippi, and close to Florence in northwestern Alabama.

This course follows an ancient trail first used by animals, and then various peoples, as it connected the southern end of the Mississippi River, through a portion of Alabama, to the salt licks available in middle Tennessee.

Since it was created by animals, it generally follows the tops of low hills and ridges, the safest and easiest route for them to travel. This avoided excessive hill climbing and the danger of getting trapped in a low-lying valley. It also allowed a watchful view of the surroundings. The gentle slopes and curves have been preserved in today's Trace.

The buffalo and other wildlife tracks were soon joined by American Indians, traders, trappers, missionaries, western bound settlers, and others as the route became more familiar. Travelers would pass through dense forests, swamps, cotton fields and hills as they made their way along.

Although getting its name from the city of Natchez, Mississippi, the Trace has been in existence for centuries. It was used by the explorer De Soto in the 1500s, but was a familiar trail to the Chickasaw and Choctaw Indians for hundreds of years prior to that.

During the late 1700s and early 1800s, it was common for farmers and boatmen to haul their merchandise down the Mississippi River to New Orleans, sell their goods and even their flatboats for lumber, and then travel the

Trace back northward by foot or horseback. Their return trip along the Trace could be every bit as exciting as navigating the strong currents of the river had been on their passage downstream.

The most boisterous group were called the "Kaintucks," a rowdy bunch of wild frontiersmen who floated down the Mississippi River on flatboats loaded with furs and other goods. They typically sold their boats and goods for cash, perhaps dallied at the Under-the-Hill entertainment venues, and

then headed back home on the Trace. While some of these men might be targeted by robbers, most of the Kaintucks were meaner than the outlaws.

If there were two or more of them together, they were likely to be scrapping among themselves, but when confronted by a would-be opponent, would band together and not hesitate to take on an army, if need be. Kaintucks were generally allowed to pass freely.

Later the Trace was even used by the early settlers moving westward during the 1800s. Always fraught with danger, the Trace was a favorite hangout for the unscrupulous members of society. With the constant danger of being robbed and/or murdered, many of the Trace travelers disappeared and were never seen again.

From early on, the Trace was filled with many hazards, such as outlaws, Indians, and wild animals, earning it the nickname, "Devil's Backbone." Traveling in groups became popular for security reasons. Since many of the people traveling north were carrying money from their sales, they were a preferred mark for the bandits. Some even made it a habit to accompany postal workers on their routes, as those workers were generally left alone. Even the devious members of society were interested in the mail getting through, as this provided most of the news from other parts of the country.

Eventually the steamboats, improved stagecoach lines, and construction of railroads made the route obsolete as far as a means of passenger and freight commerce.

There was never a straight rail line built between Nashville and Natchez, so major population centers arose elsewhere. This stunted the growth of towns along the Trace, just as being bypassed by an interstate highway did to others in later years.

The current Trace is a relatively narrow strip of land that winds its way from Mississippi to Tennessee. Just beyond the tree-lined road are many small communities with unique stories and attractions of their own. Some have annual celebrations, legendary bed and breakfast establishments, and scrumptious homemade cooking. Each historic site, wayside exhibit, and century-old structure reveals an interesting piece of our country's past.

Instead of being wary of outlaws, today the travelers along the Trace only have to beware of animals crossing the roadway, or of accidentally exceeding the posted fifty mph speed limit. The two-lane road is not meant to

be rapid transit, but is designed to be enjoyed at a slow pace. It is quite a scenic pathway, and is ideal for driving, biking, hiking, horseback riding, picnicking, and camping.

Today the Trace is a limited access highway devoted to preserving an important part of the area's history. There are parts of the original trail still accessible, and that's not all that remains from days past. There are many accounts all along the Trace of restless spirits who still appear occasionally to modern travelers. From early Indians, to explorers, tradesmen, settlers, outlaws, and others, there seem to be a number of entities who refuse to, or for some reason can't, rest in peace. These are the subjects of the stories in this book.

DOGWOOD MUDHOLE

A mile to the south, the Old Natchez
Trace crossed a depression in the flat,
dogwood-covered ridge. After heavy
rains it became almost impassable for
wagons. Its name Dogwood Mudhole
recalls the ordeals of frontier travel.
It shows too how place names arising
from local conditions of long ago are
carried down through the years.

UNITED STATES DEPARTMENT OF THE INTERIOR
NATIONAL PARK SERVICE

TRAP-DOOR SALOONS

Since the Natchez Trace begins at Natchez, Mississippi, that city will serve to be the home of our first story. The bluff on which the city was eventually built was originally more known for what lay beneath it.

Beginning in the late 1700s, a wide flat area that extended for several hundred yards from the banks of the Mississippi River to beneath that high bluff on which Fort Rosalie had stood was named "Under-the-Hill."

Due to the importance of the location as a port, a steady stream of goods flowed through the location. Loaded flatboats came down the river, their goods sold and traded for merchandise coming by ship from other countries. This financial hub resulted in the city of

Natchez being built on top of the bluff. Soon there was a distinct difference in what was found on top of the bluff and what was at the bottom.

Natchez, at the top, was home to the affluent and proper populace, while the decadent and more sinful element was at the bottom. Of course the wealth at the top depended heavily upon the success of the commerce conducted at the bottom. After the city of Natchez was constructed, that lower area's name quickly changed to "Natchez-Under-the-Hill."

Natchez-Under-the-Hill has been described as a gambler's paradise, a cesspool of depravity, and a resort for the damned. It was one of the wildest landings along

the Mississippi River. There were saloons, gambling havens, and, of course, houses of ill repute. As the farmers and boatmen sold their wares, they took advantage of an opportunity to spend a little of their money and raise a little cane before starting the long and treacherous journey along the Trace back to their homes. Unfortunately, there was abundant treachery also to be found right there by the river.

With a limited land area, there were many saloons built on stilts out over the river, known as "trap-door saloons." Naïve visitors who partook of the attractions there were sometimes clubbed, robbed, and their bodies dropped

through trap-doors in the floors of the saloons into the river below. Knife fights and killings were simply an accepted everyday incident of life in the community.

It is rumored that one of the more common ghostly sightings for the last hundred years involves the unfortunate souls dropped through those trap-doors. Strange lights and smoky wisps are frequently seen off-shore. Some people claim to have seen tortured faces in the small patches of fog; others swear that they have heard screams of agony and moans of sorrow. These sounds always come from where the small balls of light dance across the water. There have even been reports of people hearing a splashing noise before the sounds begin, as if made by something the size of a body being dropped into the water from several feet above.

The sightings are generally reported very late at night. Witnesses claim that during a calm evening, a stiff breeze suddenly kicks up, the lights and eerie sounds start immediately, and then the quiet tranquility resumes within a few minutes.

These tormented souls are assumed to be destined to forever repeat their fatal last moments, dropping to their watery grave from those trap-door saloons.

THE OUTLAW JOHN MURREL

During the middle 1800s, it was common for a person to get into trouble with the law in New Orleans, catch a steamboat up the river to Natchez-Under-the-Hill and lay low until things cooled down for them. Most lawmen considered the hideout too dangerous to enter, so it was a good haven for the bad people.

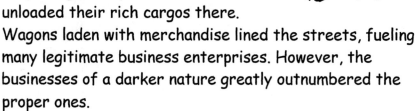

Natchez-Under-the-Hill was also an important port for deep-water voyagers and sea-going ships from all over the world as they navigated up the river and unloaded their rich cargos there. Wagons laden with merchandise lined the streets, fueling many legitimate business enterprises. However, the businesses of a darker nature greatly outnumbered the proper ones.

Today the lavishness of the wealthy class of the "Old South" is still on display high on the bluff in Natchez. There are old antebellum homes that can be toured, and souvenirs of a long ago era to be purchased. Below the bluff is a simple landing for the Delta Queen Steamboats. According to many reports, there are also things of a more sinister nature lurking along the river, as well.

One spot that seems to be haunted is close to the edge of the river. Near the main ship landing was a slave block where slave traders held weekly auctions of human flesh. This is the approximate location where people continue to witness unworldly entities.

A famous outlaw ghost presumed to be haunting the

area is that of John Murrel, an infamous dealer in stolen slaves during the early 1800s. He was reputed to have sold slaves, stolen them back, and then re-sold them over and over. Finally in 1835, fate struck back. Murrel was rumored to have started a slave rebellion in New Orleans and was lynched by an angry mob. That seems a fitting end to his appalling life.

Murrel had spent much of his time around that slave block by the river. Many stories recount his ruthlessness in dealing with the slaves. Some slaves were so afraid of him that, after he sold them, they would run away and sneak back to him, believing that otherwise he would find and torture them. His intimidation worked.

After Murrel re-sold the same slaves numerous times, occasionally buyers would recognize the familiar merchandise. Once this happened, those slaves became worthless to Murrel, so he is alleged to have simply killed them.

The ghost of Murrel, as well as possibly those of some of his victims, is frequently seen along the waterfront. His ghost sometimes is seen stomping along the grounds, making threatening gestures. Other times he is seen dangling from an invisible gallows, a noose around his neck.

The ghosts of the slaves usually wander around aimlessly, crouching in fear. Some people, however, claim to have seen them dancing joyously around the hanged ghost of Murrel. There doesn't seem to be any sounds associated with these sightings.

SWEETWATER BRANCH

This small branch receives its name from
the clean and fresh, or sweet, flavor of
its water. Thousands of years of erosion and
flooding have gradually built up the fertile
bottom lands that you see under cultivation
near here.

The branch is still carving and shaping
the valley. You may follow the struggle of
trees and other vegetation to gain a hold
in the shallow rocky soil in the bottom in
a 15-minute stroll along this nature trail.

UNITED STATES DEPARTMENT OF THE INTERIOR
NATIONAL PARK SERVICE

J. THOMPSON HARE

Although the invention of the steamboat slowed commercial traffic along the Trace, it had an opposite effect on Natchez-Under-the-Hill. Hundreds of steamboats docked at Natchez, and the rowdiness of

that area only increased. Gamblers, thugs, murderers, snake-oil salesmen, prostitutes, and traders, dealing in every illegal substance known to man, flocked to Natchez-Under-the-Hill to search for customers and/or victims. Outlaws used it as a home base from which they could ply their trade on travelers along the nearby Trace. Organized prostitution is said to have survived into the 1990s when one of the last houses of ill repute was firebombed, killing the elderly madam.

Joseph Thompson Hare was an infamous outlaw patrolling the Trace, robbing and occasionally killing his victims. Hare told of seeing many strange things along the trail, perhaps simply to intimate travelers. He reported seeing a phantom white horse numerous times.

After eventually being hanged for his crimes, people reported seeing his laughing ghost near that city he called home, Natchez-Under-the-Hill. The ghost of his mistress has also been seen nearby.

The story is that Hare began dating a girl from Natchez-Under-the-Hill, and even though she had a rather questionable reputation, he expected her to be faithful to him. He showered her with jewels that he had liberated from travelers along the Trace.

Unfortunately, his work took him away for periods of time, and the girl would grow lonesome. On arriving home one night, Hare decided that she had been cheating on him, and he flew into a drunken rage. Weighing her body down with the countless jewels he had given her, he dumped her struggling body into the Mississippi River.

There are occasional reports today of people in the area below the bluff hearing the maniacal laughter of the outlaw. Others claim to have seen the body of a young woman struggling out in the river, or her ghost floating along the river banks trying to escape her murderer or her heavy weight of jewelry.

KING'S TAVERN

Natchez-Under-the-Hill is haunted by ghosts other than the outlaw Hare. Located along the riverbank, it has sordid tales that go back to the 1700s and 1800s.

One of the oldest buildings in Natchez, Mississippi, is famous for its ghostly inhabitants. Constructed in the 1760s, the structure was purchased by Richard King in 1789 and became King's Tavern. The legend is that Richard had a serving girl, named Madeline, who conveniently also served as his mistress.

Unfortunately for Madeline, she was a fun-filled and mischievous waitress. She supposedly had eyes for more men than Richard, and he was the jealous type. Madeline suddenly disappeared, and nobody admitted knowing what became of her.

Then in the midst of remodeling during the 1930s, three mummified bodies were discovered buried in the tavern's cellar, behind a brick fireplace. Two of the bodies were males, but the third one was that of a young girl. A jeweled dagger was found next to her body.

The story takes a turn here, as the dagger was similar to one known to have belonged to Richard King's wife. One theory is that the wife found out about his affair with Madeline, then had her killed and the body bricked into the fireplace. The identity of the two males is anybody's guess. Another rumor was that Richard King caught his mistress in a transgression and dispatched all of the transgressors and hid them in his cellar.

Of course this is only supposition, but it also provides a possible explanation for what many people have reported seeing over the years. There have been hundreds of employees and guests who have encountered the ghost of a young girl in the building.

The ghost is always described as wearing a low-cut dark dress with a white apron, which was the common attire of waitresses in the tavern during Madeline's era. She is almost always laughing and acting flirtatious. The ghost has appeared all around the tavern, but most often in a room close to the kitchen.

As one witness described it, "She seemed to come right through the wall. She looked directly at me, smiled, winked, and disappeared right back through that same wall. I had this strong feeling to follow her, but ran into the solid wall. Then I swear I heard her laughing on the other side of the wall."

Workers at the tavern also report hearing the sound of a baby crying from rooms that turn out to be empty. The story that goes with this incident involves an outlaw in the area during the 1700s. A young mother was trying to comfort her fussy infant when one of the notorious Harpe brothers approached her. Instead of coming to

the lady's assistance, however, he grabbed the infant and killed it. As the distraught mother looked on in horror, Big Harpe returned to the bar and ordered another drink. This is only one of many such senseless acts of cruelty attributed to the brothers, with more on them later.

There is also a mirror in an upper floor room that is supposedly haunted. According to the staff, sometimes you can see a person's reflection in the mirror of someone who isn't in the room. It is always a man in an old-fashioned dark suit. He has a short beard, bushy eyebrows, and very piercing eyes.

A stately young man in a military uniform has been seen by various people many times over the years. He is seen both inside and outside the establishment, and seems oblivious to those around him.

Some say this entity is the ghost of an American spy who divulged secrets to the Spanish during the Spanish-American War. Ghosts of Spanish soldiers have also been reported in that same area.

Finally, one of the rooms has a bed that seems to be favored by some type of ghostly spirit. Many people have reported that when placing their hand on the bed, it has warm spots, as if someone had been lying on it. Some have claimed that they smoothed out the bedspread only to find it wrinkled a minute later.

In any event, King's Tavern is a favorite spot for anyone desiring to cavort with ghostly spirits.

HARPE BROTHERS

The psychotic Harpe brothers were known for committing bloody atrocities, including maiming and torturing their victims as well as robbing them. Not content to simply take valuables from their victims, they seemed to obtain some type of devilish pleasure in causing pain to other people. These men were the most violent and feared outlaws along the Natchez Trace.

They were known as Big Harpe and Little Harpe. Little Harpe, whose real name was Wylie, discovered that one of his gang members had a price on his head. Therefore, he cut off the guy's head and took it into town to collect the reward. Unfortunately for Little, the sheriff recognized his horse as one reported stolen, and locked up Wylie in the jail. The people in town, fed up with the senseless mayhem, decided to take matters into their own hands, and hanged Wylie. Then they removed his head and placed it in a tree on Natchez Trace as a warning to other outlaws.

A few years later people began reporting seeing some strange sights along that location. Continuing to this day, occasionally someone will report seeing a ghostly head dangling from a tree along the Trace. When investigated by authorities, no sign of the head has been found.

Others have claimed to see a headless man stumbling along the Trace, searching for his lost head. Several hikers have passed quite close to this entity, accidentally, of course, and say that he is dressed in old western garb. This ghost has even been said to be holding a cowboy hat in one hand, but has no place to put it. Legend has it that this is Little Harpe, forever roaming the Trace in search of his lost head.

UNDER-THE-HILL SALOON

Today three modern day steamboats, the Delta Queen, Mississippi Queen, and the American Queen dock at the Natchez landing. These provide an idea of how it must have been in the early days of the steamboats arriving at the Under-the-Hill port.

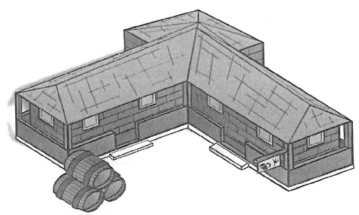

During that era of being known as a den of iniquity and home of the rowdiest scoundrels around, there were numerous saloons, gambling parlors, and houses of ill repute. While there is little left today of the area's wild history, a few vacant buildings remain. One establishment has refused to give in to the passage of time, however. It is the Under-the-Hill Saloon, and the building is over 200 years old. It is crammed with memorabilia and pictures depicting the life of that long-ago period.

Remarkably, the building is still a saloon. A visitor can only imagine what those walls have witnessed. Naïve travelers could have been scammed, robbed, and even killed there. It is reputed to have been one of the many houses of prostitution in the zenith of the steamboat days.

Today it is a mingling place for locals and tourists simply passing through, just as it was in the 1800s. Patrons have to belly up to the bar to get their drinks, as they did in the old days. While the conversations in the past might have had sinister reasons behind them, with local outlaws looking for victims, today the talk is of a different nature. Most of the tourists want to know tales of how things were in the early days of the saloon.

While most locals are well aware of the evil reputation of the region, and many have the old familiar stories to relate, there are other accounts to pique the interest of the tourists. These tales are of the supernatural happenings that have been witnessed for decades.

In that very saloon there have been several ghostly beings sighted over the years. One of the most common is apparently the ghost of a riverboat gambler. He has been seen repeatedly, standing down at one end of the bar, carefully watching the other patrons. He seems to be sizing them up, looking for one that might be drawn into a game of chance.

A number of people have turned to ask the bartender about the strangely-dressed man, only to point to a vacant spot when they look back. The end of the bar will be totally empty, with no sign of the gambler.

There has also been a female ghost seen in the saloon. She is dressed in a scanty costume reminiscent of a dancehall girl of the 1800s. She is usually near a corner and looking quite distressed. If approached, she turns to mist and disappears, although she sometimes immediately reappears in another area of the saloon.

A ragged soldier from the Civil War era has been sighted outside of the premises. A Southern infantryman, he appears to be injured, scared, and running from someone. He generally is glimpsed limping around the corner of a building, as if anxious to get out of sight.

McGLAMERY STAND

In frontier language, a stand was an inn or a trading post--sometimes both-- usually located on a well traveled route. Such a place was established on the Old Natchez Trace, near here, in 1849 by John McGlamery. Although the stand did not outlast the Civil War, the name did. The nearby village is still known as McGlamery Stand.

UNITED STATES DEPARTMENT OF THE INTERIOR
NATIONAL PARK SERVICE

THE LINDEN HOUSE

There is a bed and breakfast very close to downtown Natchez, but relatively secluded, too. The Linden House has remained in the Conner family since 1790, and is on the National Register of Historic Places. It is one of the more renowned examples of the antebellum period in Natchez. It remains popular as a fashionable site for weddings and receptions.

The east wing was added in 1818, and the house has been featured in several magazines. The front door was even copied for "Tara" in the <u>Gone With the Wind</u> movie. The home has one of the finest collections of Federal style furniture in the Old South.

There are six bed and breakfast rooms in the house with breakfast served each morning in the formal dining room. There are many attractions in nearby downtown Natchez, but there are also some items of interest on the grounds of Linden House for those of the paranormal persuasion.

There have been reports for well over a hundred years of people in the house hearing the sound of a horse and buggy pulling into the front driveway. In recent years,

there have even been some people who were sitting on the front porch who heard those sounds. Naturally there is never anything seen by these witnesses.

Other people have watched an old rocking chair on the front porch begin moving on its own. This has happened when there was not any wind stirring at all that could be blamed for the movement. The chair begins rocking, slowly at first, and then picking up speed for several minutes. Gradually it slows until stopping. Those who have approached the moving chair claim that there is a definite chill in the air immediately around the chair until it ceases its movement.

There is a piano in the house that has been heard playing an old-fashioned dancing tune in the wee hours of the morning. Whenever anyone entered the room to investigate, the music stopped abruptly, and the room had nobody in it. A couple of workers have reported hearing what sounds like a soft giggle coming from the

vicinity of the piano. If this is a ghost playing the music, it seems to be a bit mischievous.

In one of the bedrooms, a ghostly apparition of a man wearing a top hat has been seen frequently over the years. This ghost seems aware of the people around him before vanishing into a wall.

A spooky sighting witnessed by many people at least since the late 1800s involves a lady in a long dress standing on the edge of the roof of the east wing. Startled viewers see this woman flinging herself from the roof, but she vanishes into thin air before hitting the ground. No viable explanation for what this ghost represents has ever been offered. The most common supposition is that she might have been distraught over the loss of her lover during the Civil War.

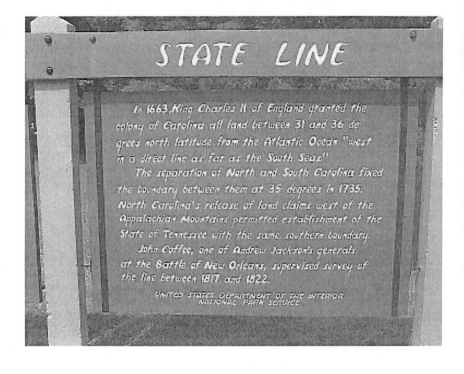

STATE LINE

In 1663, King Charles II of England granted the colony of Carolina all land between 31 and 36 degrees north latitude from the Atlantic Ocean "west in a direct line as far as the South Seas"

The separation of North and South Carolina fixed the boundary between them at 35 degrees in 1735. North Carolina's release of land claims west of the Appalachian Mountains permitted establishment of the State of Tennessee with the same southern boundary.

John Coffee, one of Andrew Jackson's generals at the Battle of New Orleans, supervised survey of the line between 1817 and 1822.

UNITED STATES DEPARTMENT OF THE INTERIOR
NATIONAL PARK SERVICE

PORT GIBSON

About halfway between Natchez and Vicksburg lies Port Gibson. As well as being close to the Natchez Trace, it is also a stop along the Mississippi Blues Trail. According to local legend, General Grant said that Port Gibson was too beautiful to burn, so it was spared during the Civil War. The town makes much use of that saying on signs and in their tourism brochures.

A significant Civil War battle was fought close by Port Gibson. When General Grant defeated the Confederates, it demonstrated the South's inability to defend the Mississippi River line, opening a path on to Vicksburg.

West of Port Gibson is the Shaifer House. It was used as both a headquarters and a hospital by each side during the Civil War. The nearby Wintergreen Cemetery contains many graves from the war, as well.

With a dwindling population of around 1700 people, many of the stores in the main section of town are now vacant.

One building of significance, however, stands proud, although a little worse for wear. It is the Trace Theater, on the corner of Main and Carroll Street, and it has been a popular part of downtown for decades.

The Trace Theater has been used in recent years as a community theater venue, as well as a nightclub. It was while a community theater when our story originated.

Back around 1988 there was a three-week run of Romeo and Juliet staged at the theater. The event was produced by the traveling Cornerstone Theater Company and many locals were cast in the play. It was during the second week that the actors began to suspect there was a supernatural presence in the building.

Several of the cast members began reporting seeing a dark figure in various parts of the theater. It seemed to appear and disappear randomly. Since all theaters are expected to have ghosts, nobody thought too much about it at first. Then one of the actors stepped around a corner by a curtain one day and came face to face with the ghostly figure. To the actor's horror, the figure was wearing a black top hat, but the hat was atop a pure skeleton head. The evil-looking grin of the skull absolutely terrified the actor, who quit on the spot.

Apparently the ghost also received a scare, because it was not seen again for the duration of that play. Later it began to appear at the theater once more, but no one has admitted getting very close to it again.

ROCK SPRING

Rock Spring Nature Trail offers you an opportunity to explore a small natural spring as it bubbles forth from the ground. Small fish dart about a deep pool created as the stream wandered through rich bottomland soil and limestone rock. Vegetation and trees change as you move through an abandoned field past the stream onto a rocky hillside.

After completing the 20-minute walk you may decide to pull off your shoes and dangle your feet in the swift cool waters.

UNITED STATES DEPARTMENT OF THE INTERIOR
NATIONAL PARK SERVICE

BESS

From around mileposts 90 to 100 the NatchezTrace travels through historic Jackson, Mississippi. There are museums, a zoo, Civil War homes, and famous cemeteries

to keep visitors busy. There is also the nearby Ross Barnett Reservoir available to water sports enthusiasts.

While there are a number of well-known ghost legends around Jackson, there is a very interesting story involving one of the oldest cemeteries around, Greenwood Cemetery. It is located at 324 George Street and was established way back in 1823.

In an area near one corner of the cemetery are some particularly old graves. One of these graves continues to have a spooky visitor, year after year.

People walking through the cemetery have spotted a dark figure, carrying what appears to be a lantern, near a certain gravesite. This figure is almost always seen in the

early morning hours, right around daylight. Those who have gotten a closer look claim that the figure doesn't appear to have feet, but simply floats along the terrain. It seems quite oblivious to anyone else about, focusing entirely upon its destination.

The figure disappears if a witness gets very close, but also disappears within seconds of being seen even if it isn't approached. It seems that it has a quick errand, does it, and returns to wherever spirits generally reside.

There is, of course, a legend to accompany this sighting. In the early 1800s a well-to-do family brought a slave woman into their home to assist the lady of the house. The mistress was frail and could not do much cooking or cleaning. In fact, as she grew older, she even needed help with dressing.

This slave woman, named "Bess," became like the right hand of her mistress. She helped her do everything in the house, and also helped her care for a large flower garden. This flower garden was dear to the heart of the mistress, and although she became too weak to tend to the flowers much herself, she delighted in sitting nearby and watching Bess work.

Bess soon became more of a friend than a worker. They were very close, and the mistress treated her like a member of the family. They would spend hours together each day, talking and laughing, simply enjoying each other's company.

The mistress grew weaker and weaker, eventually dying with her devoted companion by her side. From that day on, Bess would cut fresh flowers from the garden early each morning and take them to the grave of her mistress. Frequently she would gather the flowers while the dew was still on them, thinking that would 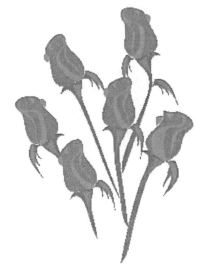 keep them fresh longer. Since this was often before good daylight, Bess usually carried a small lantern with her.

So devoted was Bess that she has continued to visit the grave of her mistress for nearly two hundred years. If you happen to be at the cemetery as daylight approaches, you might be the next witness to Bess's visit.

ROCK SPRING TRAIL

The trails and stepping
stones in this area lead you
across Colbert Creek past Rock
Spring, and through the wood—
lands. Since 1977, numerous
beaver dams have been built then
abandoned or destroyed by high
water. Walk the trails and enjoy
the changing environment of this
once free—flowing spring—fed
stream.

BRASHEAR'S STAND

At milepost 104.5 on Natchez Trace, literally across the street from Jackson, Mississippi, is the small community of Ridgeland. This is a popular tourist stop, as the nearby Ross Barnett Reservoir provides many opportunities for various outdoor adventures. There are also a number of special events and festivals in that area. In 1999, Ridgeland celebrated one hundred years, but has actually played a major role in activity along the Trace for many more years than that.

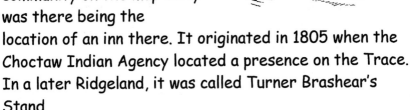

Something that put the community on the map early was there being the location of an inn there. It originated in 1805 when the Choctaw Indian Agency located a presence on the Trace. In a later Ridgeland, it was called Turner Brashear's Stand.

Turner Brashear had quite a reputation. It was he who was credited with once covertly furnishing liquor to the Chickasaws, after which they went on a drunken spree resulting in a small brawl and a dead horse. He was one of the earliest traders with the Indians, and in fact, even took an Indian wife. They had a pair of daughters who were later buried near Port Gibson. He is also reputed to have owned at least a couple of slaves, and became a

quite wealthy man for that era.

He had a stand for several years near Jackson, Mississippi, known as "a house of entertainment in the wilderness." Although he later moved to Port Gibson, his stand on the Trace continued to bear his name as late as 1825.

Around the middle 1800s Brashear's Stand was changed to King's Inn. King was a known associate of the infamous Murrel Gang, a group notorious for terrorizing, robbing, and murdering travelers along the Trace. (King's Inn was also used by General Stephen Lee as his headquarters during the Civil War.) The building became known as Hawthorne Vale until it was destroyed by fire in 1896.

Naturally such an establishment which existed for so many years in a somewhat wild environment had many stories involving its customers.

A popular legend involves hidden treasure. One version claims that the Murrel Gang hid some of their stolen loot on or near the premises of King's Inn. On familiar terms with the owner, the outlaws saw the area as a secure place to conceal some of their money for safe keeping. Rumors are that several gang members had individual

hiding places, not even trusting each other. Since some of these outlaws were killed or imprisoned, some stashes of the hidden wealth were never retrieved.

This ill-gotten treasure is credited with the presence of ghostly beings at that location. Eerie apparitions have frequently been reported roaming the area for a hundred or more years. Several treasure hunters using metal-detectors have been chased from the location where the inn once stood. Some people claim that the ghosts of the outlaws still protect their bounty.

Ghosts of another type have also been seen. These spirits seem more intimidated than intimidating. According to folklore, these spirits are from the innocent travelers to the inn who were robbed and killed for their money. They continue to dwell in the "in-between," still bewildered by their unexpected demise.

CAVE SPRING

The description of the ground surface
and the type of rock indicate that this
cave was a result of solution activity. A
long room or corridor was dissolved out of
the rock by under-ground water. The roof of
the room eventually weakened and collapsed.
Indians may have used this site as a source
of water and stone. The water is now unsafe
to drink and the cave is dangerous.

UNITED STATES DEPARTMENT OF THE INTERIOR
NATIONAL PARK SERVICE

THE LEGEND OF RUNNING DEER

Located at milepost 160 is the friendly town of Kosciusko, Mississippi. It is known for its greenhouses and gardens, a favorite stop for bed and breakfast fans, and, incidentally, the birthplace of Oprah Winfrey. There is also a walking and driving tour of the downtown area called Towers and Turrets, with several inviting eating places around the square. For our purpose, however, the major claim to fame for the town is its close proximity to Natchez Trace.

There is a particular area on the nearby Trace where the ghost of a young Indian woman has been reported being seen for well over a hundred years. The majority of the sightings have occurred in the vicinity of milepost 160.

Typically a traveler along the road will suddenly see this young woman standing at the edge of the forest, staring intently into the distance. The lady looks quite real, and perhaps distressed, so many of the viewers have stopped to see if they can be of assistance. They think perhaps she is lost or is with someone who has become injured.

It is only when the witnesses approach close to the Indian that she appears to notice their presence. Acting alarmed, the woman usually backs into the cover of the forest. The next thing the would-be rescuers observe is a deer where the woman was last seen. The deer looks

directly at them for a couple of seconds, and then bounds rapidly away, disappearing from sight quickly.

The astonished witnesses return to their vehicles, and the realization slowly sinks in that they may have just witnessed a ghost.

There are several theories concerning the ghost of the Indian woman. The most popular is that she is a product of the common "lost-love" legend. For whatever reason, a young Indian woman loses her true love. This is sometimes from being betrothed by her father to another young brave. She commits suicide rather than marry the brave who she doesn't love.

In this particular case, the common story is that the woman's true love was killed in battle. She waited at the edge of the village for his return, but only his horse made its way back from the battle.

The woman continues her vigil at the side of the Trace, still searching for her returning love. Exactly why her spirit turns into a deer isn't clear, other than the unconfirmed account that her name was either Running Deer or Evening Fawn.

This spirit has been witnessed so frequently over the years that a "deer-crossing" sign was erected near the spot she has been reported being seen most often.

THE HAUNTED COINS

With all of the wagon, boat, and ship traffic, Natchez was an important gateway to the wild, uncharted west. The city became a supply store and gathering place. As the furthermost southwestern outpost of the United States, it became a natural launching spot for many

historic expeditions. There were scientists, explorers, soldiers bound for the Texas and Mexican Wars, and others simply seeking their fortune and adventure.

Serving as the link between the goods of the North and the trading ports of Mississippi and Louisiana, the area also attracted other types of people. There were settlers heading west, various traders, explorers, the lawless highwaymen, and a host of itinerant preachers.

An area with such a varied influx of people and their money, or desire for it, naturally attracted a lot of attention. There are always those who are anxious to separate the affluent from their possessions, whether by legal, questionable, or downright illegal means.

All of this resulted in a lot of nervous people who, after selling their wares, headed north along the Trace. Aware that robbers could be around the next bend or grove of trees, it was common for these travelers to hide their money when they stopped for the night. They were at their most vulnerable when camped, so their money was safest when not on their person.

Many travelers buried or hid their money at the edge of their campsites. If confronted by robbers during the night, they could show that they had little of value on them. It was common to keep a small sum with them, hopefully to appease the outlaws. Then, if they were allowed to live, they could retrieve their money as they broke camp the next morning.

Since some of the robbers weren't easily appeased, unlucky travelers did not always live to recover their hidden valuables. This is why rumors have strongly suggested that there is much loot still hidden along the Natchez Trace.

One favorite legend involves a Trace employee working in the vicinity of milepost 180 near French Camp. While cleaning up after a storm where a large, dead tree had

blown over, he discovered a leather pouch entangled in the tree roots. Gingerly opening the pouch he found it full of gold and silver coins, all of which were minted before the Civil War.

The worker took the pouch home with him that night. He hadn't mentioned it to anyone, and he wasn't sure what to do with it.

A few hours later the worker was shocked from a deep sleep by a dazzling display of lights. As he sat up in bed, he watched in amazement as balls of light seemed to be bouncing all around the bedroom. Gradually he realized that the orbs were coming from the pouch he had left on the floor in a corner of the room.

The man was finally shaken to his senses as he saw that the orbs were setting fire to various items in the room. Within seconds, the room was ablaze, and the man barely managed to escape before his entire house was engulfed in flames.

By the time help arrived, the house was a total loss, except for one item. The man recovered the pouch of coins from the ashes of his house. The pouch was not even scorched, and the contents were still intact.

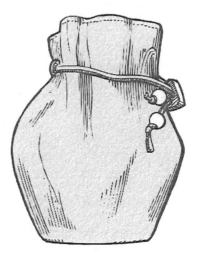

Late the next day the man returned to the spot where he had found the pouch. As close as he could, he dug a hole where the tree had been and dropped the pouch into it. Then he carefully covered up the spot with sticks and brush, leaving no sign of where he had returned the treasure.

According to the rumors, that money pouch is still setting there, waiting for the next brave soul to find the haunted coin cache.

THE ROCKING CHAIR

There are some famous cemeteries at several of the towns along the Trace, such as at Jackson, Natchez, and

Tupelo. There are also many less famous cemeteries near Natchez Trace as it passes by various communities. Some of these are close enough to be visible from the Trace, at least during the winter when leaves are off the trees.

There has been an intriguing ghostly sighting between mileposts 200 and 220 that has been attributed to spirits from one of these small cemeteries close by.

In this case, visitors traveling along the Trace are surprised to suddenly see an elderly man sitting just off the road, apparently watching the traffic pass by. This man isn't just sitting on the ground, however, but is in a wooden rocking chair, rocking contentedly.

The man has been described as having a full beard, and sometimes wearing a hat, but not always. Most witnesses say he is wearing overalls, such as a farmer might wear.

There is a strange twist to the sightings, however. At times, only the chair is seen setting by the side of the road. Although nobody is in or around the chair, it is rocking away all by itself.

Nobody knows whether the man's ghost is not always visible, or if the chair itself is haunted and enjoys watching traffic pass by, with or without its companion.

Naturally the man and the chair fade away if the witnesses stop to investigate. Generally they are reported to change into a gray fog, and then totally disappear. There is never a mark on the ground where they were spotted, as these spirits obey a common camping slogan of "Leave It Like You Found It."

WITCH DANCE

South of Tupelo, Mississippi, stands a National Park sign that simply reads, "Witch Dance." Supposedly witches gathered there to dance in their sordid rituals, and wherever their feet touched the ground, the grass died and refused to grow back. Indians and superstitious

travelers carefully avoided crossing these particular areas.

These spots are mentioned in several Civil War reports, including the judicious need to avoid them. There were diplomatic insinuations that things occurred and were observed there quite out of the ordinary. Even Andrew Jackson mentioned these spots in his journal after he made a trip along the Trace on a trip to Tennessee.

Bare scorched spots remain there to this day, and there continue to be unusual events witnessed and reported every so often by visitors to the area.

One of the most common incidents involves sounds. Many people have reported hearing screams and cackling laughter emitting from the ground near the spots. Although no ghostly beings are seen, there have been accounts of people feeling cold spots or a cool breeze blowing on them as they stand near the spots. A feeling of "something" close by is frequently described.

Others have actually seen visual evidence of something unusual going on there. People have reported seeing bluish wisps of smoke hovering over the spots. Some have seen balls of fire darting back and forth overhead. There have been several reports of just the head of an ugly woman

floating over one of the spots. She has been described as having an unforgettable wicked smile on her face that continued to haunt them. Her eyes were shining as bright as laser beams, and it was impossible to look directly at them. The feeling of being in the presence of intense evil was overwhelming, causing the witnesses to leave the area as quickly as possible.

Of course most visitors to the spots do not see anything out of the ordinary, but almost all of them will admit that looking at the area leaves them feeling a bit uneasy.

TUPELO TERROR

There are lots of tales concerning buried treasure along Natchez Trace, but one is particularly captivating. As the story goes, an elderly man on vacation from a northern state was traveling along the Trace. He stopped at one of the "points of interest" along the road to take a break from driving. While there, he pulled out his metal detector and went wandering off, killing time more than anything else.

When the detector abruptly went crazy, the man returned to his truck for a shovel. He soon unearthed an old glass jar full of gold and silver coins. Not sure what he should do, the man buried the jar back where he found it.

At one of the visitor centers, the man stopped and inquired as to the legal aspects of finding treasure along the Trace. He was told that treasure hunting was illegal, particularly using a metal detector. Anything found would belong to the government, and there was zero chance of any finder's fee.

While that irritated the gentleman, he was as honest as the day is long, and was not about to take anything that didn't rightfully belong to him. On the other hand, he saw no reason to tell the officials where he had discovered the glass jar. He decided that if it had been there for over a hundred years, it could stay another hundred.

Several years later, the man's health declined suddenly. A couple days before his death, he told the story of finding that glass jar of old coins. The closest thing to a location he gave was that it was "near the Old Trace."

Unfortunately for seekers of the treasure, there are several areas designated as the "Old Trace." One is at milepost 10 just north of Natchez, but there are others around milepost 200 close to Jeff Busby, at milepost 222, milepost 270, 375, 395, and others.

Some of these are close to visitor centers where the old man could have stopped to inquire about the legal ramifications of finding treasure along the Trace. The truth is, nobody is sure where the glass jar of coins may be buried.

The closest thing to a clue is something the old gentleman is reported to have said on his deathbed. When he related the story of finding the coins and the reception he received from the authorities, he vowed that he would come back after death and haunt the spot, making sure that nobody ever found the coins again.

There have been a number of reports over the years of people encountering a surly man dressed in dark clothing as they hiked along the edge of the Trace. Usually they were only slightly off the road, in the edge of the trees when this man abruptly appeared. Although he didn't actually threaten them, his appearance and his demeanor were sufficient for them to decide to vacate the premises. Several witnesses claim that when they looked back, the man simply disappeared. More than one also mentioned feeling a cold wind in the vicinity of the man.

All of the similar reports of this encounter have occurred near milepost 270, near Tupelo, Mississippi. Some have even called the figure "The Tupelo Terror."

AT THE BOTTOM OF BEAR CREEK

There were inns, or stands, as they were called, all along the old Natchez Trace. Unfortunately, some of these places did not provide the safe refuge that the travelers sought. Staying overnight at some of them was more dangerous than traveling the Trace itself.

Lone visitors traveling north were in the most danger. Many such people stopped at a stand for the night and were never seen or heard from again.

There was one particular stand near the Tennessee River that was known to be a good source for bridles, saddles, or wagon parts. It was widely accepted, but seldom mentioned, that these items had been "liberated" from unfortunate clients of the inn.

The inn was heated with wood, and the woodpile behind the main building usually had several pieces of lumber recognizable as parts of carts or wagons.

Another stand, near Bear Creek, was also known as a place where people sometimes never left. It had a reputation of serving the cheapest liquor on the Trace. The reason given for this was not because of their generosity, but more for their curiosity. After plying a

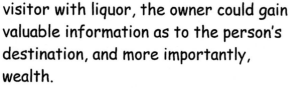

visitor with liquor, the owner could gain valuable information as to the person's destination, and more importantly, wealth.

Gaining the victim's trust, the owner would sometimes offer to secure the traveler's valuables for "safe keeping," or perhaps discover where the people had hidden their money before coming to the inn.

Many clients of the inn woke up the next day with a headache and no money. Those were the lucky ones. Others never woke up at all, but wound up chained at the bottom of the creek nearby.

To this day, there are parts of the creek where locals refuse to go swimming. There have been too many stories and rumors spread about what lies beneath the water there. Some people claim to know instances when swimmers felt boney hands grabbing their ankles, either trying to drown the swimmers or pull their own skeletal bodies to the surface.

There are also stories of people diving down into the deeper part of the creek and coming face to face with one or more grinning skeletons chained at the bottom of the water.

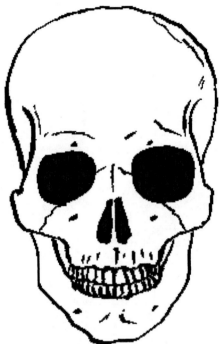

After the creek flooded a few years ago, there were also reports of human bones found at various places downstream. This was followed by a rash of claims of seeing ghostly skeletons around the creek. These beings seemed to be moving helter-skelter, as if searching for their rightful place.

Other witnesses reported hearing moaning and wailing sounds near the creek, but not seeing anything to have caused the noises. That is why locals simply choose to avoid that portion of Bear Creek.

BEAR CREEK MOUND

The village site was occupied as early as 8000 B.C. by hunters who stayed only long enough to prepare their kill. From the time of Christ to 1000 A.D., migratory people of this area practiced limited agriculture. The nearby fields and streams offered an abundance of nuts, fruits, game and fish. These people shaped this mound and built a crude temple on its summit to house their sacred images.

UNITED STATES DEPARTMENT OF THE INTERIOR
NATIONAL PARK SERVICE

THE MARRIAGE TOWN

Back in the 1950s, some of the small towns in Mississippi had a somewhat naughty reputation, particularly those within close proximity to the state of Tennessee. It was the law in Tennessee that there was a three day waiting period between obtaining a marriage license and the actual marriage ceremony. The theory was that might give people time to rethink their actions, lest they launch themselves into a hasty deed they might later regret. Mississippi, however, had no such restriction. Industrious youngsters quickly caught on to the fact that they could cross the state line into Mississippi and get married immediately.

Thus, several northern Mississippi towns became known for quickie marriages. Young people in love could sneak off to Mississippi and be married before their folks knew what was happening. These towns brought dismay, joy, or despair, depending on whether the recipients were distressed parents or frustrated young lovers.

Corinth was notorious for being one of those legendary small Mississippi towns. Setting barely across the state line, it became a popular destination for eloping young Tennessee couples bent on getting married without having to wait three days or get permission from their parents.

Although Corinth is actually thirty something miles from

Natchez Trace, it is nevertheless connected to a famous ghostly haunting along the Trace. This is due primarily to it being a favorite spot for those quick marriages.

A young couple from Waynesboro, Tennessee, had fallen head over heels in love. They were only seventeen, still in high school, and needed their parents' permission to get married; something neither set of parents was willing to give. They felt that the couple was too young and needed more time to grow up prior to making such a lifelong commitment. Thus was born the necessity for a scheme.

One Saturday, the girl was scheduled to go on a picnic at Pickwick Dam, near Savannah, Tennessee. This was a little over twenty miles north from Corinth.

Meanwhile, the boy was supposedly going hunting in the woods east of Waynesboro. Instead, he stopped by a friend's house, changed clothes, and drove to Natchez Trace. He planned to drive down the Trace to US Highway 72, hop over to Corinth, meet his girl, and get married.

The girl had arranged for a friend to sneak her down to Corinth and check into a motel. There she would wait for her future husband.

The careful planning started, and eventually ended, without a hitch, so to speak. The girl made it to the motel, changed into the white dress she'd planned to wear for the wedding, and waited for the boy. She waited and waited and waited, but he didn't show up.

The hours slipped slowly by, and in due course the day turned into night. Still she waited, and still there was no sign of the boy. She paced the floor and cried, getting more and more upset. When dawn arrived, and still no groom, she became convinced that he had gotten cold feet and had backed out of the arrangement. Certain that there was no way she could face the embarrassment of the situation, and believing that her one true love had turned his back on her, the distraught girl committed suicide.

Almost immediately after the tragic death, there were strange sightings at the motel. Many people reported seeing a girl in a white dress peering out of the window of one of the motel rooms. The bizarre thing was the room was really always vacant. Even workers at the motel would clearly see someone at the window, but upon checking the room, there was never anyone there.

At other times the girl in the white dress was seen outside the door, or even in the parking lot. She was always staring down the road, as if anticipating seeing someone approaching. Then, as quickly as she appeared, she would fade away into nothing.

Even after the motel closed down, the girl would still be seen occasionally, most often at a window. When the motel was demolished, the people thought that would be the end of the sightings. Instead, the ghost moved down the road. At the eastern edge of Corinth stands a large sign, welcoming people to the city. The girl in the white dress has been seen standing, or sometimes sitting, beside that sign, staring eastward toward Natchez Trace. She seems forever doomed to wait for someone

who will never come.

Meanwhile, let's go back to that fateful day of the planned elopement. The boy had started south on Natchez Trace, dressed in his best clothes, almost overwhelmed by the anticipation and excitement of marrying the love of his life.

What happened next was never known for certain. The common supposition was that perhaps a deer, or some other animal, ran across the road in front of his car. In any event, the car swerved off the road and down a slight embankment into the woods. The car slammed into a large tree, killing the young boy instantly.

Due to thick bushes and the fact that the car traveled past several small trees, the vehicle was not readily visible from the road. It was the following day before the frantic parents found out most of the details of the

planned elopement, and another day before searchers discovered the boy's body in the wrecked car. By then the girl's body had also been found, so it was a double tragedy.

Within a few weeks, there were reports of travelers along the Trace seeing a distraught young man in a dark sport coat standing along the edge of the road. He didn't really seem to be aware of the passing traffic, but appeared to be looking for something. If the travelers stopped their vehicles, the young man slowly faded away and disappeared.

Many years have passed, but this particular apparition continues to be reported occasionally on Natchez Trace around milepost 340.

GHOSTLY CORINTH

There are other stories told around Corinth. The city was home to a major Civil War battle, and at different times there were houses occupied by both sides. These houses were utilized as hospitals, headquarters, and for both official and unofficial rest and recreational ventures.

In the 1990s a couple moved into a two-hundred year old house that had served as a hospital during the Civil War. The upstairs had been used as a surgical ward, and several of the floors had dark stains that could not be washed away. Even when the floors were painted, the stains would reappear within a few days.

One day while the husband was away on business, the wife heard the sound of someone walking around upstairs. From the irregular sound of the steps, she surmised that the person was either limping or dragging one leg along.

Summoning all of her courage, as well as arming herself with a shotgun, the lady crept up the stairway, but the closer she got to the top of the stairs, the fainter the sounds became. Although she thoroughly searched the upstairs rooms and closets, there was no sign of anyone in the place.

No sooner did she return downstairs than the walking sounds began again. The lady stood at the foot of the stairway, listening to the sounds drawing slowly nearer. Then the stepping seemed to be starting down the stairs, but there was nobody to be seen.

The lady fled from the house and steadfastly refused to ever return to it. The house was immediately put on the market.

BUZZARD ROOST

The entrance to the Trace at milepost 320 is known as Buzzard Roost. First known as Buzzard Sleep, the name was changed to Buzzard Roost in the early 1800s by Levi Colbert, who lived nearby. The spring there provided the Colbert family with water. Levi was an enterprising Chickasaw chief whose home was an inn, or more commonly called a "stand" in those days.

The stand was a popular place for travelers along the Natchez Trace. They were made to feel welcome in a friendly atmosphere and were fed quite well, too. About two hours away by horseback was a stand run by Levi's brother, George. Together they ran Colbert Ferry, which provided transport across the Tennessee River. There might have been a friendly rivalry of sorts between the two brothers and their stands. According to the gossip, George sold whiskey at $1.00 a bottle, but Levi undercut him and sold it as low as twenty-five cents, trying to lure thirsty travelers to his inn.

Today this is one of the scenic stops along the Trace. There are exhibits there describing the Colbert family,

Chief Levi Colbert, and the spring. There is a short, but challenging trail with steep steps down to the spring itself. (I once visited it just after a rain, which made the damp trail even more challenging. There was a light misty haze lingering over the water, but I didn't think much about it. Later I heard a tale involving such a fog at the spring that made me wonder how close I came to my own encounter.)

Since the late 1800s there have been occasional reports of strange events around the spring area. Visitors to the spring have claimed to see unexplained images hovering about the water. These accounts vary from witnessing a very life-like person who fades away to nothing, to briefly seeing a person's face in the water, to a cloudy mist which seems to have a life of its own. A few people maintain that they were actually touched by a ghostly being, swearing that icy hands grabbed them by the arm or leg.

One lone visitor to the spring was standing at the edge of a pool when suddenly an arm shot out of the water and

grabbed the person's ankle. With the arm seemingly intent on dragging the victim into the pool, it was only with an extreme effort that the person was able to pull free. Although the water was quite shallow at that point, and the bottom was easily seen, the person could not see the arm, or anything else, in the water. Needless to say, that was the end of that visit.

The mysterious sightings around the spring continue to this day. Early one morning after overhearing a couple of tourists mention something spooky at the edge of the water, a Trace employee decided to check it out. Here is a tale that he purportedly told friends:

"It was early in the morning, and being a week-day, the visitors had been sparse. After the couple drove away, I walked down to the spring to see for myself what they were talking about.

The spring sets kind of low, and there will sometimes be a little fog there when there isn't anywhere else. This was the case that morning. As I climbed down the rocky trail to the spring, I felt the fog envelope me. The temperature seemed to drop about ten degrees within that fog. Now I'm not easy to spook, but suddenly I

began to hear a whispering sound. I knew I was the only one around, but it sounded like a couple of people whispering to each other, or to me. I immediately got chill bumps all over my body.

The fog got thicker for a few seconds, and then it thinned back out, but I could still only see maybe eight feet in front of me. Suddenly a small patch of the fog grew darker, and it slowly transformed into the shape of a grown woman. It was more like an outline, with virtually no distinguishable features, but it did have long flowing hair that seemed to be tossed about by a breeze.

I stood there paralyzed in a state of shock, and that cloudy figure moved right up to me. It felt like the

temperature dropped another ten degrees. While the form roughly maintained the shape of a woman, I could still see right through it.

About that time I came out of my shock, and I'll admit that I turned and scrambled up that trail as fast as I possibly could. I never looked back, even when I reached the parking lot, as I was afraid that form might be following me. I'd never believed in ghosts, and don't know for sure that I do now, but that thing was not anything of this world as I'd always known it. I've not gone down to that spring by myself since then."

There have been other reports related to when there was an early morning fog hovering around the spring. Perhaps the fog emboldens the spirits to emerge from their hiding places to seek their revenge, rescue, answers, or whatever purpose they have.

It is known that several parties were ambushed at the spring, as it was a common stop for people traveling along the Trace. There have been theories that the spring is haunted by some of those victims, or maybe the ghosts of the attackers remain there, still waiting for their next victims. Others say that it could be the ghost of Levi Colbert, himself, lingering at his spring, either protecting it or trying to entice another guest to stay at his inn.

COLBERT FERRY

George Colbert operated a ferry that crossed the
Tennessee River from around 1800 to 1819. He also had a
stand, or inn, to provide Trace travelers with a place for

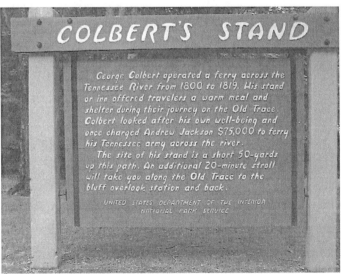

a warm meal and shelter. Colbert is notoriously
remembered for charging General Andrew Jackson
$75,000 for moving his Tennessee Army across the river.

Today there is a visitor's center and a couple of short hiking trails, as well as picnic areas overlooking the river. It provides current travelers a nice rest spot, with considerably less danger involved than in Colbert's days.

Colbert was described as shrewd, self-serving, wicked, and other such terms. He was half-Chickasaw and helped negotiate with the U.S. government on the Indians' behalf.

George had a brother, Levi, who had his own stand nearby, and they often competed for clients. One way was to provide cheaper liquor, although both were often accused of watering down their whiskey.

Like many other stand owners along the Trace, George was reputedly not past taking advantage of his customers for his own personal gain. One story concerns a man coming back from Natchez, his saddlebags loaded with gold. He purchased a cheap horse for the journey back north to Kentucky.

When he got to Colbert Ferry, he was quoted a high price for carrying him and his horse across the river. The two men got into a heated argument, but Colbert refused to lower the price for using his services. The suspicion is that George was eyeing those bulging saddlebags, and had a good idea what made them bulge. Colbert thought that he had the man without an option, and would not negotiate at all.

George underestimated the man and his stubbornness. Those acquainted with the gentleman knew that he had always been extremely tight with his money. Not wanting to pay Colbert's price, the man decided that he and his horse could swim across the river at that point. Unfortunately, the horse was already worn out by the trip and struggled in the water after getting only about fifty yards from shore.

One account had George Colbert going out in his ferry to the struggling duo and offering help. The rumor was that Colbert asked the man to hand the saddlebags of gold up to him, but the man refused, not trusting George.

In any event, the man would not turn loose of his saddlebags and wound up sinking, along with the horse. The story became known as Jeb, his gold, and his horse. As the legend grew, it was known as gold and horse, and finally "the golden horse."

The man and his horse's body eventually were found, but not the saddlebags. The gossip was that Colbert knew exactly where they went down, and might have possibly recovered the gold for himself.

Regardless, there has been a ghostly sighting along the river there for many years since. Witnesses report seeing a horse's golden skeleton head rise above the water, stay visible briefly, and then disappear back into the depths of the river.

Some say the horse's ghost is still fighting to not drown, while others say the spirit is guarding the gold-laden saddlebags, still submerged in the murky depths of the river.

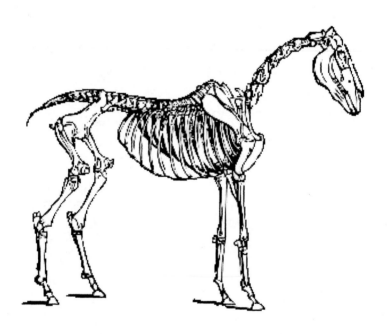

SUNKEN TRACE

There are several places along the Trace referred to as the "Sunken Trace." Over many years of thousands of

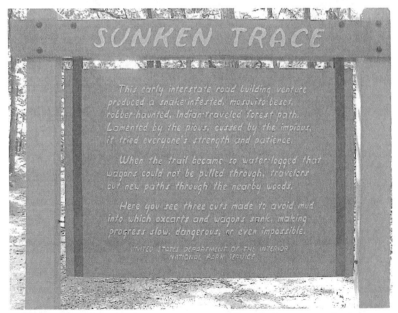

SUNKEN TRACE

This early interstate road building venture produced a snake-infested, mosquito-beset, robber-haunted, Indian-traveled forest path. Lamented by the pious, cussed by the impious, it tried everyone's strength and patience.

When the trail became so water-logged that wagons could not be pulled through, travelers cut new paths through the nearby woods.

Here you see three cuts made to avoid mud into which oxcarts and wagons sank, making progress slow, dangerous, or even impossible.

UNITED STATES DEPARTMENT OF THE INTERIOR
NATIONAL PARK SERVICE

people, animals, and wagons traveling along easily eroded soil, the path gradually wore down into gulley-like trails. Some of these spots are close to the current paved

Trace, and are easily accessible to the travelers. This provides a view of the original pathway as well as affording a hiker the opportunity to walk in the very steps of many who traveled the Trace in centuries past.

There are sunken portions marked near Saltillo, Mississippi, Port Gibson, Mississippi, and Waynesboro, Tennessee. There are legends associated with at least two of the spots.

At milepost 350 the Sunken Trace has had a permanent resident for well over a hundred and fifty years. A tall dark figure has been seen from the paved road, but more

frequently it has been encountered by hikers walking along the nearby sunken path.

Usually witnesses have looked ahead to see a dark presence among the trees beside the trail. It seems to be a male, and is typically described as wearing a hat and long coat such as worn by travelers in the early 1800s. Most people do not get close enough for a clear view, as the figure fades away into nothing as they approach it.

A few people have claimed that they were sufficiently near to see a snarling, menacing expression on his face. Some even claim that he made an aggressive motion with one arm toward them prior to disappearing. One man alleged that the figure walked toward him in a threatening manner. This hiker quickly retreated rather than have a close encounter.

There are several theories as to the reason for this ghostly presence. One is that it is the unhappy ghost of a businessman who was killed by outlaws as he made his way to his northern home. One version was that he had buried his money when he made camp for the night. Although tortured by the outlaws, he didn't divulge where his money was hidden. His ghost still guards that money.

A slightly different version is that the ghost is an outlaw who was killed by the businessman. The northern gentleman continued homeward, and the outlaw ghost is still angry at his failure, continuing to haunt the scene of his unexpected end.

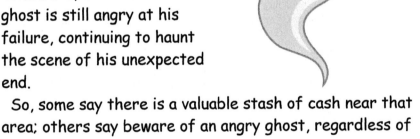

So, some say there is a valuable stash of cash near that area; others say beware of an angry ghost, regardless of its origin.

HOME OF DAVID CROCKETT

At milepost 370 Natchez Trace crosses over U.S. Highway 64. A short sixteen miles east is the town of Lawrenceburg, Tennessee, home to several interesting

legends of the ghostly persuasion. One of the town's claims to fame is that David Crockett moved there in 1817 and made it his home. There is a large statue of Crockett on the south side of the square, commemorating his importance to the county's early beginnings. This monument was erected in 1922 and stood a mere ten feet from the old courthouse. Contrary to the television series and its theme song, there is apparently no evidence that anyone, friend or foe (of which he had many of each), ever called him "Davy," and he would have likely taken offense if they had.

Crockett was known to frequent the Natchez Trace during his travels, and its close proximity to Lawrenceburg might have played a large part in his settling in the town for a while.

He served as a justice of the peace, a colonel of the militia, and later a state representative. Crockett was also an industrialist, building a powdermill, a gristmill, and

a distillery along the banks of Shoal Creek. At the time, many mills were built along creeks in Tennessee for the water power. Unfortunately, these creeks would occasionally flood, wiping out the mills. After having his mills destroyed for the second time, Crockett moved on to West Tennessee in 1821, where he was elected to Congress in Washington. He later died at the Alamo Mission in Texas in 1836.

David Crockett State Park was officially dedicated in Lawrenceburg in 1951, honoring the pioneer, soldier, politician, and businessman. Since then, the park has constantly been improved, and lives up to its reputation of being about the nicest and most popular park in Tennessee. With its miles of hiking trails, campsites, restaurant, pool, and other amenities, it welcomes thousands of visitors annually. Since it is virtually situated in the town, it is also utilized regularly by the local people, too.

There is a David Crockett Museum, furnished with various items from the Crockett era. During the early days of this museum,  workers noticed that there were certain items that would not stay put. The items would be left in one place each night, but then would be in another location the next morning. After this occurred numerous times, and the items were always found at the same spot, workers decided to leave them alone. The items were not moved again, as apparently "someone" wanted them in a certain place.

There have also been reports of people seeing a shadow in the museum. It has appeared moving across the floor and along a wall. The problem is that there is never a person there to cause that shadow. Witnesses claim that the shadow appears to be that of a woman in a bulky dress, such as those worn many years ago. Nobody has come up with any viable suggestion as to who this ghostly shadow might be, although many think it may be connected to some of the artifacts in the museum.

LAWRENCE COUNTY JAIL

About a block and a half west of the Lawrenceburg town square is the former jail house. It was built in 1893 and used until 1973. Currently it is the Old Jail Museum,

containing memorabilia from its many years as the county jail. The main cellblock was upstairs, with the sheriff and his family living in quarters downstairs. Fortunately, it has an intriguing ghostly legend.

In January of 1943, Sheriff Cleve Weathers went upstairs to a jail cell containing a drunken prisoner. At this point, there are several versions of the story, none of which may be entirely truthful. One version claimed that the sheriff went into the cell to break up a fight. Another version is that he went into the cell to question a prisoner. There is even a version that he hit the prisoner in order to subdue him. All versions agree, however, that the prisoner pulled a concealed knife and stabbed the sheriff repeatedly.

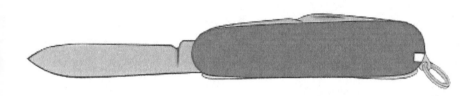

The mortally wounded sheriff staggered from the cell and collapsed into the arms of a very large highway patrolman standing there. His last words were, "He cut me bad."

As the dying sheriff was gently lowered to the floor, another lawman quickly stepped around them and slammed the cell door closed. He didn't shut the door to keep the prisoner in, but to keep the highway patrolman from going into the cell. This act was widely recognized as saving the prisoner's life for a trial, and perhaps saving the highway patrolman's career, as well.

Sheriff Weathers was a well-respected man of the community, and his murder sent a shockwave throughout the county. There was an emotional trial, and the killer was sentenced to serve ninety-nine years in the penitentiary. This was a much talked about subject for years thereafter, but also had another side-story.

According to a family member of a sheriff who later lived in the jail building, they would occasionally hear the metallic sound of a cell door being slammed shut overhead. Investigation would find nobody in the upstairs, but the door of that particular cell where the former sheriff had been stabbed was inevitably found closed. This incident always occurred when no prisoners were in the cellblock, so there was no easy answer to how the cell door slammed shut. They would also sporadically hear the sound of a man's low moaning cry coming from the empty upstairs.

These noises occurred so frequently that the family learned to simply ignore them. Although the incidents weren't widely mentioned publicly, the family did warn the following sheriff of what to expect.

The man who killed the sheriff was released after serving fifty years of his sentence. He died three years later, and there have been no reports of the strange noises since that time.

Old Jail Museum (rear view)

THE WRECKED VW

In the middle 1960s there was a head-on car wreck near the Trace. It was a rainy night and the accident happened around midnight. A young Lawrenceburg woman in a Volkswagen was trapped in the wreckage and burned to death before help could arrive. With the gas tank in the front, the early VW Beetles were notorious for catching fire during front-end collisions. The burned hulk of the car was towed to a wrecker  storage yard. Typically, such a wrecked car is kept until an insurance agent can investigate and sell the wreckage to the highest bidder for salvage. This action usually takes anywhere from a week to a month, depending on the agent's schedule.

The night following the wreck, a man living next to the storage yard was rudely awakened around midnight by the  short, shrill cry of a woman. He described it as a scream of sheer terror, but searched and could find nobody in distress. He claimed that the cry seemed to come from the vicinity of that burned vehicle.

This alarming incident happened three nights in a row, leaving the man quite shaken. Sometime during the fourth day, the car was hauled away. Nobody ever admitted knowing who moved the car or where it was taken, but the man never heard the scream again.

LAWRENCE COUNTY COURTHOUSE

The old courthouse on the Lawrenceburg square was built in 1905. This majestic old building was deemed too expensive to repair and was replaced in 1974 with a new

one built west of town. There was much discussion concerning the destruction of the landmark building, but it was eventually torn down. There are still strong feelings concerning this event on both sides.

The building had quite a history, and was witness to many interesting happenings. On the north side of the courthouse stands a monument to the men (known as the "Lawrenceburg Blues") who served during the Mexican-American War in the middle 1840s. It is one of only two such monuments in America. This monument is credited with being the reason the Yankees did not burn the original courthouse during the Civil War. Their leader, Major Gibbon, was afraid that the resulting blaze might damage the nearby monument. This fact preserved much of the county's historical papers stored in the building.

The courthouse was also witness to many political disagreements, altercations, and downright abuses. One such incident involved missing ballot boxes. There was a typical hotly-contested county election. The normal procedure was for the ballot boxes in all of the county precincts to be sealed and brought to the courthouse for the official counting. The vote count frequently lasted late into the night, and it was common for a large crowd to gather around the square, waiting for the final results. Election Day was also a reason utilized by many as an excuse to imbibe of the spirits. In fact, it was widely reputed that many votes were swapped  for bottles of liquor on voting day. Thus, it was to be expected that a number of the people gathered around the square were a little tanked, and heated discussions and fights were common.

During one such election night, someone allegedly climbed through a window of the courthouse and absconded with some vital ballot boxes. The votes in those boxes were expected to be heavily in favor of one particular side, and could affect the outcome of several races.

The missing boxes were later found, empty and discarded. There was only one unreliable witness as to who stole the boxes. The man considered by many as the likely thief turned up dead a few days later. The case was investigated quickly by newly elected authorities and

ruled a suicide, even though the man was rumored to have been shot in the back of the head with a rifle.

There were reports for many years afterward of people seeing a dark figure of a man climbing through a certain courthouse window. This was the same window that the ballot box thief used. If chased, the figure would immediately dissolve into nothing. Ghostly figures seem to have the ability to appear and disappear at will.

According to rumors, there was one man in particular who saw the ghostly form many times. It was as if the apparition was purposefully showing itself to this person. This man happened to be from a group in the legal profession who profited greatly from the theft of those ballot boxes. He was also one of the main forces behind insisting that the old courthouse be torn down.

OLD COURTHOUSE CLOCK

A familiar portion of the old courthouse has its own story. Setting high on top of the building was a large four-sided clock. For decades the local townspeople

listened to the chiming of that clock to count down the hours of the day. When the courthouse was torn down, the clock was kept somewhat intact and transported to a maintenance area at David Crocket State Park, where it still remains.

There are campgrounds near the maintenance area, and occasionally a camper will mention being awakened in the

wee hours of the morning by a clock chiming four times. There is a more modern clock at the park, near the swimming pool, which does actually chime. However, the campers seem certain that the sounds that they hear are from the opposite direction, toward the maintenance area, and the chimes have a distinctively different tone than the clock by the pool.

Nobody has come up with an answer as to how that old courthouse clock could possibly chime any more. There is also no good theory on why the ghostly chimes always signal four o'clock in the morning.

GHOSTLY MOTEL

One of the first motels in Lawrenceburg was built on the east side of town along Highway 64. It consisted of several individual stone units, several of which still stand there today, a testament to their sturdy construction. Although it was an attractive motel, the units have not had a customer for more than a half century. At least,

 they haven't had a live customer.

There are rumors concerning this strange vacancy that have been passed around among the town's children for decades. The stories were generally mentioned around Halloween, as the children dared each other to go into the motel units.

One legend concerns the location of the motel, which is very close to one of the town's oldest cemeteries. The story is that restless ghosts from the cemetery gather in those empty motel units at certain times, such as at midnight on nights with a full moon. People claim to have heard shrill screams and scary laughter coming from

those empty buildings. When investigated, of course, there was never anyone to be seen.

There is another interesting legend connected to the motel which has been told in quiet circles for these many years. That version involves the use of those motel units as a popular rendezvous spot for some of the leaders of the community to consort with women having questionable morals.

According to the gossip, there was an altercation in the late hours one night, and a woman wound up dead. There was a lot of activity at the motel for several hours, with several prominent people scrambling to save their reputations. The girl had worked as a waitress at a local tavern and not been in town for long. The death was quickly declared a suicide, and claiming no immediate kin could be found, the undertaker hastily buried the woman in a pauper's grave.

Sometime later, when actual kinfolk of the woman did appear in town, they could not get any information concerning the death. Nobody would admit knowing exactly where the woman died, and the undertaker couldn't remember precisely which cemetery he took her for burial.

When the relatives tried to get a court order, a local judge was not cooperative at all, as he was rumored to have been right in the middle of the incident.

Now the ghost of the dead woman allegedly continues to haunt the unit where she met her untimely death. There have been many reports of people seeing a woman's distressed face at one of the windows, and at times a shadowy figure of a woman moving around inside one of the 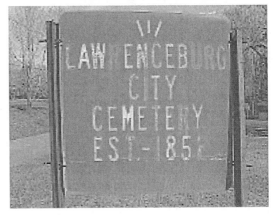 units. When the unit is checked, naturally there is never anyone to be found.

One of the mysteries of the motel is why it has never been torn down, even though it has not been used for so many years. Perhaps the ghostly inhabitants protect it? There seem to be more things buried around the town than what is found in the cemeteries.

WAS IT "THE" FRANK JAMES?

Lawrenceburg may be most famous for its connections with David Crockett, but the county isn't a one-trick-pony by any means. Before the Wright brothers flew their plane in North Carolina, there was a Mr. Pennington who

lived in the northern part of Lawrence County. In 1877, he patented a working model of an "aerial bird," which he claimed was a flying machine, and received quite a bit of publicity.

Unfortunately, Patterson died around that time, but that isn't the end of his story. Immediately after his death, two strangers appeared, inquiring as to his residence. They reportedly went to his home and convinced his widow to sell them all of his designs and drawings. Rumors were that they were from North Carolina.

Also, the notorious James Gang was known to have roamed into Tennessee. Both Jesse and Frank worked in Nashville at times while waiting for things to cool down in Missouri. Later there was a Frank James who settled in the southeastern part of Lawrence County in the Appleton community. He had a farm and even taught at a nearby school. Several times the neighbors noticed that Mr. James had mysterious visitors, and he occasionally disappeared for weeks at a time.

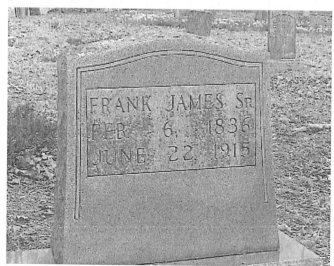

There were strong suspicions that he was "the" Frank James, but he caused no trouble locally, and people weren't overly nosey concerning his business affairs. Upon his death he was buried in a small cemetery near there, where a tombstone bearing his name still stands.

Over the years there have been many reports of people passing by that cemetery and seeing a figure dressed in black standing near Frank's tombstone. If the witnesses went back to check the cemetery, the figure was always gone. The figure has been described as that of a small man wearing a black hat, and also that of a woman in a long black dress and wearing a black hat and veil.

It isn't clear if there is only one figure or two that haunt the cemetery. Apparently nobody has ever gotten a real close look, as the figure vanishes into thin air.

INDIAN AT NAPIER MINE

At milepost 382 on the Trace is the location of the Napier Mine. It was an open pit mine which provided ore for some of the iron-making operations in that area. John

Catron was the driving force behind the mine during the 1820s and 1830s. (He later became the Associate Justice of the United States Supreme Court.) The mine actually was named for his predecessors, the Napier family.

There is a stretch through the western side of Lawrence County, extending into Lewis County where the ridges are rich in iron ore. In fact, there is a town in southwestern Lawrence County named "Iron City."

The type of iron ore is limonite, which is sometimes referred to as brown ore. Depth of ore varies along the ridges, ranging from fifteen to sometimes sixty feet. The Napier Mine was still producing ore at a depth of forty-five feet.

The furnaces were originally fueled by timber, of which there was a vast quantity all around the area. Thus, the stripping the top of the soil and cutting large number of trees resulted in a virtual raping of the landscape.

This attack on nature is what is credited with the appearances of the so-called Guardians of Nature, the Native Americans. The first incident was reported to occur in a dream. A foreman at the mine had an Indian brave appear to him in his sleep, scolding him for what was going on at the mining operation. The man did not tell anyone about the dream until a second incident happened

a few weeks later. One of the workers looked up and saw an Indian on horseback, standing at the edge of the woods. The Indian just sat there and stared at the worker for a long period, and then slowly disappeared.

The worker excitedly told others about what he had seen, but nobody paid any attention to him until the foreman caught word of it. He questioned the worker, and privately decided that it fit the description of the brave in his dream.

When other employees began seeing the Indian, the word of the first worker was vindicated. It was always an elderly Indian in native garb, sometimes on a horse and sometimes simply standing nearby. Inevitably he would slowly fade away as the people watched.

Several men got spooked by the apparition and quit their jobs. One laborer whose task was to cut timber turned in his axe, claiming that every time he started to swing it at a tree, the Indian appeared in front of him. He decided to work somewhere else.

One theory at the time was that the Indian spirit was simply trying to protect the land from the abusers. There was also a claim that the mine operations were taking place at the location of a major Indian burial ground. This version alleged that many bones and artifacts were unearthed during the excavations at the mine. This might have awakened the Indian spirit, whose task was to keep watch over the gravesites.

Although there were no records of the spirit actually doing physical harm to anyone, the sightings continued for many years. No doubt there were some sleep disturbances caused by the sudden appearances and disappearances, attested by the number of people who abruptly quit their jobs there.

Production at the mine declined in late 1800s when a high grade Bessemer ore was discovered in the Lake Superior region. It was immense deposits that could be mined at a much lower cost than the mines in Tennessee.

Gradually, as the mine area was abandoned, nature slowly but surely reclaimed the land. Today there are few visible signs of the massive destruction. Of course there is still much ore in the ground there. With improved technology it may one day become cost effective to re-open the mines in that area. I'm sure the Indian spirit certainly hopes not!

STEELE'S IRON WORKS

Here, about 1820, stood a charcoal-burning furnace used to manufacture pig iron. All that remain of this pioneer enterprise are a slag pile and the evidence of a mill race, used to bring water from Buffalo River to operate the furnaces air blasting machinery.

MERIWETHER LEWIS

After the end of the Lewis and Clark Expedition in 1806, Meriwether Lewis was appointed Governor of the Louisiana Territory. He didn't enjoy the job for long, as he didn't like sitting at a desk all day. Much of his time was spent dealing with politicians, abuses with the fur trade and problems with land titles.

Meriwether Lewis 1774-1809

He soon became involved in a feud with Frederick Bates, as the man began spreading vicious rumors about Lewis, and undermining his authority. Lewis' personal life began to unravel, too, as land speculation wiped out much of his finances. His vouchers for medicine for the Indians were not being paid by the government, and his health began to fail. In this scenario, Lewis decided to travel to Washington and attempt to straighten out a lot of the corruption he witnessed in dealing with the Louisiana Territory and defend the charges that had been leveled against him.

Meriwether planned to travel down the Mississippi River to New Orleans, and then by boat to Washington, D.C. Upon reaching the Chickasaw Bluffs, near what is now Memphis, Lewis heard that the British were in the Gulf of Mexico, so, fearing capture, he decided to travel by land to Washington. The route took him along the Natchez Trace, which was a wild and treacherous wilderness trail at the time.

Although in ill health, Lewis set out with two pack mules for his records, some servants, and Major John Neely, the Cherokee Indian agent at the Bluffs. Already plagued with a terrible headache and a fever, Lewis soon ran into a heavy storm. The pack mules scattered, and the servants went in search of them. Major Neely persuaded Lewis to ride to a nearby home and rest, promising that he would help find the important records that the mules carried.

Thus, Lewis wound up at the home of John Grinder, called Grinder's Stand, which served as an inn for travelers along the Trace. Mr. Grinder was away on business at the time, but Mrs. Grinder let Lewis in and prepared a meal for him. Soon thereafter the servants arrived with the mules. Mrs. Grinder reported that Lewis ate very little, and was quite agitated. He paced the grounds, ranting about his enemies in Washington. She prepared a bed for him, but he instead made a pallet on the floor with a buffalo robe. The servants were sent to sleep in the barn, and the Grinder family went to bed.

Mrs. Grinder reported that she was awakened several times during the night by the sound of Lewis pacing the

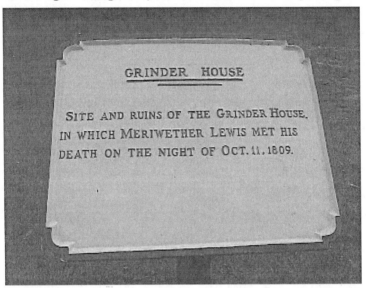

GRINDER HOUSE

SITE AND RUINS OF THE GRINDER HOUSE, IN WHICH MERIWETHER LEWIS MET HIS DEATH ON THE NIGHT OF OCT. 11, 1809.

floor and talking, presumably to himself. In the middle of the night she heard a gunshot, and something heavy falling to the floor. Then she heard the words, "Oh, Lord!"

Almost immediately there was another gunshot. Then she heard Lewis' voice at her door, saying, "Oh, Madame, give me some water and heal my wounds." Mrs. Grinder was too scared to leave her room and assist him. Some two hours later she sent her children to the barn to inform the servants. They came inside and found Lewis on the floor with a wound in his side and in the head. He died around dawn.

Major Neely arrived later that morning and took charge of Lewis' papers. He carried them on to Washington, and all of the protested vouchers were immediately paid. All of Lewis' journals were turned over to the State Department and presumably stored.

The following year, John Grinder was brought before a grand jury and accused of Lewis' murder, but the charges were dismissed because of a lack of evidence or motive. Lewis' death was declared a suicide, but with so many questions unanswered, many historians are quite suspicious. Why didn't Mrs. Grinder try to assist him? Why didn't the servants hear any sounds of gunfire? What about the people who had a lot 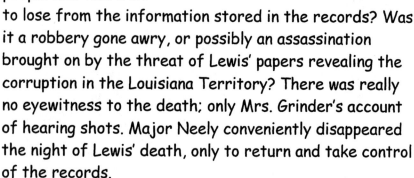 to lose from the information stored in the records? Was it a robbery gone awry, or possibly an assassination brought on by the threat of Lewis' papers revealing the corruption in the Louisiana Territory? There was really no eyewitness to the death; only Mrs. Grinder's account of hearing shots. Major Neely conveniently disappeared the night of Lewis' death, only to return and take control of the records.

Meriwether Lewis was buried on the property, which is near the current town of Hohenwald, Tennessee. This land is now the Meriwether Lewis State Park, at milepost 386 along Natchez Trace. But the story refuses to die quietly. There are legends that the ghost of Lewis continues to occupy the area where he met his death.

One story is that the sound of a metal dipper rubbing against a water bucket is often heard on dark rainy nights near Lewis' gravesite. The restless ghost of Lewis may still be trying to get water to soothe his fever and cleanse his wounds. Witnesses say the sound seems to be very close, but there is never anything seen that could be the source of the noise.

There is a tall monument at one end of the park, with a circular drive going around it. There have been many

reports of people seeing a dark figure kneeling at the monument. The figure is seen from a distance, but when approached, the figure simply disappears.

A log cabin contains artifacts and newspaper articles about Meriwether Lewis, his life and exploits. Visitors have heard a man's voice seeming to come from a corner of the cabin, when nobody is there. The voice has been described by different people as sounding quite distressed, moaning, or ranting excitedly. There have been some witnesses who thought they heard the words, "Oh, Lord," or "...so hard to die."

THE NATCHEZ BRIDGE

Approaching the northern end of the Natchez Trace, at milepost 438, is an engineering marvel. A bridge over Highway 96 west of Franklin, Tennessee, proved to be a major highlight of the Trace.

The bridge was designed by Figg Engineering Group and

constructed by PCL Civil Constructors. The 1572-foot bridge was opened in 1994. The double arch bridge is designed to place most of the weight on those two arches.

A lady in a long white dress has been spotted from time to time on the bridge. Witnesses are surprised to suddenly see a woman standing at the side railing. They are even more astonished to see the woman climb over and disappear from the bridge.

There are at least two versions of why this apparent

spirit haunts the bridge. In one version, a man was supposedly killed during the early construction of the bridge. His death occurred only a few days before he was scheduled to get married to his high school sweetheart.

His fiancé, completely distraught over the loss of her true love, was sent away by her parents on a trip to Europe in hopes of giving her an opportunity to overcome her grief. Upon her return, she seemed a different person, and appeared to have gotten her life back on track. Although she still grieved, it seemed to be under control.

Sometime later, after the completion of the bridge, she started the habit of driving out onto the bridge and tossing a single rose over the side. Then one day, on the anniversary of the death of her fiancé, she drove her car out to the middle of the expanse, parked, and threw herself over the side.

Another version involves a teenage romance. The girl became pregnant, much to the consternation of her family. Her father, a prominent member of a local law firm, was quite irate when he discovered her condition.

The young man, meanwhile, panicked and joined the military. He promptly left town, not wanting such a permanent commitment with his life.

The girl, as in the first version, went out on the bridge and committed suicide. Her family, still trying to save themselves from ridicule and embarrassment, managed to cover up the suicide. Instead, it was ruled an accidental death.

In both versions, the spirit of the dead girl continues to appear on the bridge periodically. She seems destined, or determined, to relive the last seconds of her life. Perhaps she hopes the ending will be different.

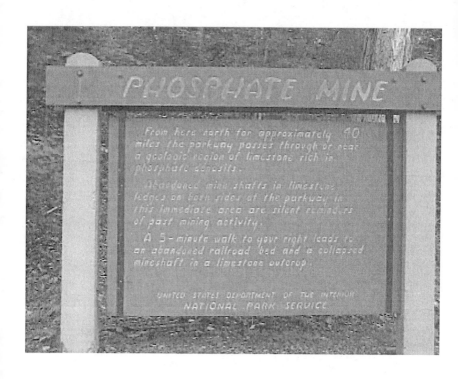

PHOSPHATE MINE

From here north for approximately 40 miles the parkway passes through or near a geologic region of limestone rich in phosphate deposits.

Abandoned mine shafts in limestone ledges on both sides of the parkway in this immediate area are silent reminders of past mining activity.

A 5-minute walk to your right leads to an abandoned railroad bed and a collapsed mineshaft in a limestone outcrop.

UNITED STATES DEPARTMENT OF THE INTERIOR
NATIONAL PARK SERVICE

EPILOGUE

My first memory of Natchez Trace goes back to the early 1950s. Our church youth group made several trips to the Trace for picnics. The Trace was only sixteen miles west of town, and then a couple more miles south to a great picnic area. The spot had restrooms, numerous picnic tables, grills for cooking hamburgers, and a small stream of water passing through it.

There was a Nature Walk that traveled a little way along the stream and through the woods. The stream was shallow enough for wading and splashing each other. There was  also a plaque that explained a little about the Natchez Trace and its importance as a major trade route, and later for Civil War troop movements. (The Civil War involvement piqued my interest sufficiently for me to eventually visit the Shiloh Battlegrounds outside nearby Savannah, Tennessee.)

A few years later, when I began dating, Sunday afternoon drives were a popular activity. The Natchez Trace was a natural location for such dates. One could cruise along the quiet roadway, have a picnic along the way, and hike along some of the many short trails at the scenic sites.

Skip a few more years forward, and I had moved to Texas. I discovered that the drive to and from Tennessee to visit my folks was much less hectic when I made part of the Trace a portion of my return trip. If I

had time to spare, I could get on the Trace at milepost 370 and stay on it all the way to Jackson, Mississippi. Even with less time, I could drive down the Trace and get off at Buzzard's Roost and cut through Corinth, Mississippi. Over the years, I have driven the middle portion of the Trace many times, stopping on various trips at each of the historic sites for a brief rest.

Thus, when I began writing this book, I already knew a great deal about my subject. These insights proved valuable in knowing which nooks and crannies to poke into with my research. Such familiarity with a topic always makes the writing much more interesting to me, and hopefully allows me to describe the subject matter in a manner to make it more interesting to the readers, as well.

AUTHOR'S BIO

Much of my impressionable youth was spent (or misspent) in the hills, valleys, and creeks of Middle Tennessee. Although I didn't realize it at the time, I was absorbing tales and experiences that served me well in  the writing of this book. I can't remember not being fascinated by the supernatural and mysterious things around me. From comic books to scary movies, my imagination was honed early and later fine-tuned to the areas of nature that could not be easily explained or dismissed.

Nevertheless, I led a somewhat normal work-life until I fell in with the unruly computer crowd. Computers are as supernatural as one can get. They can do marvelous things with incredible speed, although not always exactly what their programmers desire or expect. I discovered very early that computers do in fact have a will of their own. They behave differently when unattended or when only one person is around them than they do when two or more people are present. That is a simple fact, attested to by anyone who has had much experience working with them.

People who think they can totally control a computer are only fooling themselves.

Thus, I have maintained a love-hate relationship with computers since my first indoctrination with a room-sized, vacuum-tube-driven monstrosity that vaguely understood a language known as Autocode.

After many years of combat in industrial, research, and military applications, I finally realized that computers are smarter than programmers, and I've declared a truce. I still use them, but it is like riding a rebellious horse; you can hang on and enjoy the ride, but don't always know for sure where you'll wind up.

Some of the work that I and/or my computer have managed to complete can be found at:

www.larryhillhouse.com

GHOSTS OF INTERSTATE 90 Chicago to Boston by D. Latham

GHOSTS of the Whitewater Valley by Chuck Grimes

GHOSTS of Interstate 74   by B. Carlson

GHOSTS of the Ohio Lakeshore Counties by Karen Waltemire

GHOSTS of Interstate 65   by Joanna Foreman

GHOSTS of Interstate 25 by Bruce Carlson

GHOSTS of the Smoky Mountains by Larry Hillhouse

GHOSTS of the Illinois Canal System by David Youngquist

GHOSTS of the Niagara River by Bruce Carlson

Ghosts of Little Bavaria   by Kishe Wallace

Shown above (at 85% of actual size) are the spines of other Quixote Press books of ghost stories.
These are available at the retailer from whom this book was procured, or from our office at 1-800-571-2665 cost is $9.95 +
$3.50 S/H.

Ghosts of Interstate 75   by Bruce Carlson

Ghosts of Lake Michigan   by Ophelia Julien

Ghosts of I-10   by C. J. Mouser

GHOSTS OF INTERSTATE 55   by Bruce Carlson

Ghosts of US – 13, Wisconsin Dells to Superior   by Bruce Carlson

Ghosts of I-80   David youngquist

Ghosts of Interstate 95   by Bruce Carlson

Ghosts of US 550   by Richard DeVore

Ghosts of Erie Canal   by Tony Gerst

Ghosts of the Ohio River   by Bruce Carlson

Ghosts of Warren County   by Various Writers

Ghosts of I-71 Louisville, KY to Cleveland,OH   by Bruce Carlson

GHOSTS of Lookout Mountain by Larry Hillhouse

GHOSTS of Interstate 77 by Bruce Carlson

GHOSTS of Interstate 94 by B. Carlson

GHOSTS of MICHIGAN'S U. P. by Chris Shanley-Dillman

GHOSTS of the FOX RIVER VALLEY by D. Latham

GHOSTS ALONG J-35 by B. Carlson

Ghostly Tales of Lake Huron **by Roger H. Meyer**

Ghost Stories by Kids, for Kids by some really great fifth graders

Ghosts of Door County Wisconsin by Geri Rider

Ghosts of the Ozarks B Carlson

Ghosts of US - 63 by Bruce Carlson

Ghostly Tales of Lake Erie by Jo Lela Pope Kimber

GHOSTS OF DALLAS COUNTY   by Lori Pielak

Ghosts of US - 66 from Chicgo to Oklahoma   By McCarty & Wilson

Ghosts of the Appalachian Trail   by Dr. Tirstan Perry

Ghosts of I- 70   by B. Carlson

Ghosts of the Thousand Islands   by Larry Hillhouse

Ghosts of US - 23 in Michigan   by B. Carlson

Ghosts of Lake Superior   by Enid Cleaves

GHOSTS OF THE IOWA GREAT LAKES   by Bruce Carlson

Ghosts of the Amana Colonies   by Lori Erickson

Ghosts of Lee County, Iowa   by Bruce Carlson

The Best of the Mississippi River Ghosts   by Bruce Carlson

Ghosts of Polk County Iowa   by Tom Welch

Ghosts of Ohio's Lake Erie shores & Islands Vacationland by B. Carlson

Ghosts of Des Moines County   by Bruce Carlson

Ghosts of the Wabash River   by Bruce Carlson

Ghosts of Michigan's US 127   by Bruce Carlson

GHOSTS OF I-79   *BY BRUCE CARLSON*

Ghosts of US-66 from Ft. Smith to Flagstaff   by Connie Wilson

Ghosts of US 6 in Pennslyvania   by Bruce Carlson

Ghosts of the Lower Missouri   by Marcia Schwartz

Ghosts of the Tennessee River in Tennessee   by Bruce Carlson

Ghosts of the Tennessee River in Alabama

Ghosts of Michigan's US 12 by R. Rademacher & B. Carlson

Ghosts of the Upper Savannah River from Augusta to Lake Hartwell by Bruce Carlson

Mysteries of the Lake of the Ozarks   Hean & Sugar Hardin

To Order Copies

Please send me _____ copies of *Ghosts of Natchez Trace* at $9.95 each plus $3.00 for the first book and $.50 for each additional copy for S/H. (Make checks payable to QUIXOTE **PRESS.**)

Name _____

Street _____

City _____ State _____ Zip _____

QUIXOTE PRESS
3544 Blakslee Street
Wever IA 52658
1-800-571-2665

To Order Copies

Please send me _____ copies of *Ghosts of Natchez Trace* at $9.95 each plus $3.00 for the first book and $.50 for each additional copy for S/H. (Make checks payable to QUIXOTE **PRESS.**)

Name _____

Street _____

City _____ State _____ Zip _____

QUIXOTE PRESS
3544 Blakslee Street
Wever IA 52658
1-800-571-2665